Millionaire Fastlane: Conquering Fear and Self Doubt that Holds You Back

By

Praveen Kumar & Prashant Kumar

Disclaimer

The advice contained in this material might not be suitable for everyone. The author obtained the information from sources believed to be reliable and from his own personal experience, but he neither implies nor intends any guarantee of accuracy.

The author, publisher and distributors never give legal, accounting, medical or any other type of professional advice. The reader must always seek those services from competent professionals that can review their own particular circumstances.

The author, publisher and distributors particularly disclaim any liability, loss, or risk taken by individuals who directly or indirectly act on the information contained herein. All readers must accept full responsibility for their use of this material.

All pictures used in this book are for illustrative purposes only. The people in the pictures are not connected with the book, author or publisher and no link or endorsement between any of them and the topic or content is implied, nor should any be assumed. The pictures are only licensed for use in

Table of Contents

Introduction

Having the desire to create wealth is only the first step in the right direction to become rich. The seed to creating wealth – that you have planted in your mind – has to be given the right nourishment to grow. It has to sprout, become a plant and then grow into a strong tree that will bear fruits of wealth for you. It is vulnerable initially to many negative forces from within and outside. We have to protect and nurture it through the initial stages.

Why Fear is your Biggest Enemy

That fear festering in your mind is the biggest threat to the seed of wealth creation that you have planted in your mind; it is like a weed that has to be removed before you can succeed.

Fear is a distressing emotion aroused by impending danger, evil, pain, etc., irrespective of whether the threat is real or imagined.

Fear is a hard-wired emotion, triggered by our subconscious. As human beings, we naturally fear everything that is unfamiliar to us and anything from our past that has resulted in feelings of pain. These feelings signal our brain, which drives our actions in such a manner that causes us to avoid pain at all costs. We will instinctually go to great lengths to prevent circumstances that bring about fear and the stress that is created within us through that fear.

We are afraid of fear because we are afraid of pain. This creates a very real problem for us, in that, we are instinctively driven away from just about everything that would result in the creation of our own financial independence.

Fear will always overwhelm everything that might bring about real change in our lives- it is unavoidable. It is in the nature of our brains to protect us from pain unless we make a conscious choice to achieve greater reward than the resulting pain brought about by what we fear.

DOUBT, FEAR, and ANXIETY are the three demons that bring our progress to an abrupt halt, right at the point when we are about to make a decision that has the potential to change our lives. Doubt creeps in and causes the fear, which in turn, causes the anxiety. The three can strike at lightning speed and freeze our decision-making capacity.

The demon of fear is, without a doubt, the biggest obstacle in our minds that does not allow us to nourish the seed of wealth. It is the fear of failure of losing all that we have achieved so far. It is the fear of criticism and ridicule. It is the fear of losing love and respect of our near and dear ones. It is always this irrational fear that holds us back from achieving greatness and financial success.

What is the Source of Fear?

What is it that causes us to freeze and lose our senses, rationality and the power to act? The primary cause of this debilitating demon is ignorance. Knowing this truth will set us free. That, in itself, is a beautiful truth.

You must understand that there is only one thing to be set free from and that is ignorance. If you analyze carefully, it is always the lack of knowledge, and the understanding of things and situations that causes fear. Let me explain: prior to the age of Enlightenment, thunder and lightning, like most unknown forces, were misunderstood and proved to be a source of great fear in the minds of people. Tumultuous nights usually scared people out of their wits, they did not comprehend what was happening. They would believe the Gods to be angry and felt guilty of their wrongdoings. It left a very deep impression of fear on their minds.

These days when science has explained the true nature of thunder and lightning, occurrences and fluctuations in weather do not cause any anxiety or fear in our minds. It leaves no impression whatsoever. We go about our daily works as if nothing has happened. It is a non-event. *Fear burns in the fire of knowledge*. Likewise, if you have the right financial knowledge, you will not suffer from fear of failure.

Similarly, our fears predominate due to the layers and layers of wrong inputs and impressions stored in our subconscious. These impressions were formed as a result of the education system that was designed in the industrial age: designed in an age where only few were privileged and the rest were trained mentally and professionally to be at their service.

Our parents and teachers, whom we loved and admired, were part of the same education system. They unknowingly passed the same knowledge down to us: become professionals, become doctors, engineers, accountants and lawyers. Get a job in a good company, work hard and be successful. No one taught us to be wealth creators. No one taught us the skills to be wealth creators.

Even the media, influencing public opinion profoundly, is a product of that old thought. We can't blame them. They were educated in the same school of thought as most of us. They imbibed the fear of God into us. The economy is going downhill. Next year, there will be a recession: they rattle rising unemployment figures, oil prices, inflation rate, foreign debt, national debt and make comparisons with the great depression of the thirties, when everyone seemed to have lost their homes and jobs.

Fear, greed and sensationalism sells—rationality does not. No doubt we're so afraid! Who would like to jump on to the bandwagon of uncertainties? Why take risks when you can get a decent job and survive? Fear is programmed in our memory chip in form of a blueprint that dictates our financial lives.

How to Overcome Fear?

We have to erase and rewrite that program if we have to succeed. Knowledge helps us to examine these fears and erase them from our systems.

Now look at the facts: our mindsets were created in a world that was poor. This was a time when there was a distinction between the privileged and the poor. These economic positions in life seldom changed. Either you were born rich or you worked for the rich. This has all changed now.

The world is moving forward at an unprecedented pace. Despite the doomsayers' prediction by the media, the world is on a projected trajectory of great material advancement. You have to just assess history, starting from the industrial revolution, to understand the financial progress made by mankind. This pace has accelerated in the past 50 years and will increase in manifolds as the information age progresses.

There might be slight aberrations but the writing is on the wall for anyone to see. The wealth of the world is about to explode as never seen before—

are you going to be a part of this expansion or get left behind?

At present, there are less than 0.1% wealth creators on this planet. This is going to change very rapidly because this advancing information age makes it possible to impart knowledge. Are you ready to acquire that new knowledge that will burn your fears and set you on path of great wealth?

Expand Your Mind State

You have made a decision to become an enlightened wealth creator; else you would not be reading this book. This is great...but be warned! Your inner nature is very powerful and strong; it is fortified by millions and millions of past impressions.

Our minds are like an elastic band: if the new force is not applied, it will try to snap you back and restore to its original position. You will need to keep applying the pressure of knowledge and burn your fears till you break free.

This is the stage where permanent transformation takes place and you do not go back to your original position. It is as though the rocket fueled by knowledge puts you into outer space beyond the pull of gravity. There is a saying that, "***Once your mind expands it never goes back to its original state.***" You will have to keep applying the pressure of Knowledge incessantly, till you find yourself in an expanded state of mind.

A rocket burns 90% of its fuel during its take off stage: once it defies gravity, very little energy is needed to keep it running. The same is true for a mind that wants to grow to an expanded state to create wealth.

All information that is recorded in our memory passes through a processor in our minds before it is recorded. The previously stored data that is recorded in our systems interferes with the processor as it analyzes incoming data. We have the capacity to change our blueprint by first erasing the old blue print by burning it in the light of new knowledge.

As the old data gets progressively removed from our systems, its interference reduces, and the capacity of our mind's processor improves. The process is very slow as there are layers and layers of files accumulated in our system. Some of these are like viruses that continuously affect the capacity of our processor to analyze data correctly.

It is a catch 22 situation: our processors are affected by the same files it is trying to analyze, which makes the task very slow and tedious. However, we can make a quantum jump in our processing capability by upgrading our processors, by increasing our financial, emotional and spiritual intelligence.

Financial Intelligence

An intellect that is honed financially helps one see opportunities that they otherwise would have not. These opportunities are seen with the mind. An unknowing fool will throw a gem away thinking it is another stone; a wealth creator will see an opportunity to make money which an untrained mind cannot see.

Financial Intelligence is the third eye which opens doors to opportunities where none exist. It creates new opportunities. That is why they say 'rich invent money.' An untrained mind, on the other hand, can create extreme poverty that lasts generations by teaching it to their families.

Financial intelligence not only creates wealth, it sustains it. There are innumerable stories of professional sportsmen who made millions during their playing years only to become bankrupt within a decade. Mike Tyson, a heavyweight champion, is one such example. He earned millions during his lifetime but is now bankrupt.

You must have also heard about lottery winners who are back to where they started within five years of winning the lottery ticket.

I was recently reading an article on the descendants of Hyder Ali and Tipu Sultan who are today penniless. They are members of families who ruled over half of India few generations ago. Why is it that these families lost their wealth? There are other families who not only sustain but grow their fortunes over generations.

The world changes, markets go up and down, technologies change, economies boom and crash. The families who survive are those that make the efforts it takes to develop their financial intelligence, which allows them to adjust to the changes and also helps find new opportunities to succeed in this changing world. They also take the trouble to teach and transmit this intelligence to their younger generations and hence, are able to sustain their wealth for generations to come.

What is Financial IQ?

There are many facets of financial intelligence. It is about understanding assets and liabilities, capital growth and cash flows, passive income as against earned income, good debt and bad debt and making money work for you instead of you working for money. It is also about tax savings and protecting your assets including intellectual property rights.

Let us examine some of these aspects in greater detail.

Assets and Liabilities

An asset, as explained by Robert Kiyosaki in his book 'Rich Dad Poor Dad', is something which puts money into your pocket and liability is something that takes money out of your pocket. By this definition your house, car, boat, golf set and other luxury items that you buy (thinking they are assets) are in actual fact liabilities. All these so-called assets take money out of your pocket. Most of these depreciate in value (except may be your house,) and are high maintenance items that cost money out of your pocket.

Most of us think that we are buying assets, but in actuality, we buy liabilities that keep us poor. This does not imply that one should not buy these things that make us feel nice and good about life: one must buy them only once sustainable wealth has been created by first purchasing income-producing assets.

The real assets are businesses, investment properties, shares, bonds, etc., that put money into your pockets and also appreciate in value. To create wealth is to buy income producing assets such as real estate, businesses and paper assets.

Capital Gain and Cash flow

Wealth is created through a combination of capital growth and cash flow. Capital growth creates long-term wealth whereas cash flow sustains it in the short term and a balance between the two is needed to sustain and fuel the growth.

Short-sighted people only go for cash flow to fund their current needs. On the other hand, there are long-term investors (especially those who invest in properties) who get into serious trouble by not understanding the importance of cash flow. A sensible combination of the two is needed to grow financially.

Good Debt and Bad Debt

People are scared of taking debt for business expansion and investments as it causes a lot of stress. At the same time, they are not afraid of taking loans to buy cars or to go on a holiday.

Financially intelligent people know that creating debts for buying income-producing assets is a prerequisite for growing rich. A good debt is when money is borrowed to create money. Just like the bank: banks take money deposits from us at a lower interest rate and loan it back to businesses or for purchasing properties at a much higher interest rate. They make money on the difference, as can anyone.

The simple trick is to borrow cheap and create an asset that pays more. Bad debts are the ones that you borrow at high interest rate and use for buying assets that depreciate or produce less, or no income.

Make Money Work for You

The best definition that defines being rich is: "*In case you stop working today because of ill health/ accident or voluntary retirement then for how long will your savings sustain your current life style*." In some cases, it may be just a few days or at best a couple of months- this means you are poor.

In other cases, it may be a couple of years. A tad better situation but is certainly not a healthy one! You will be rich if you can sustain your lifestyle adjusted for inflation, indefinitely.

The super-rich can not only sustain their present lifestyle but they make it better, and also have surplus income to reinvest so that their net wealth increases with each passing year.

This can only happen when you have a large component of your money coming from passive income in the form of rents from commercial/ residential real estate, dividends from shares, intellectual property rights or interest earned from deposits. In other words, it is money working for you even when you sleep or are on holiday. In case of a job, the money will stop flowing the moment you stop working.

Saving on Taxman's Dollars

You may or may not realize this, but the most outflow of money from your pocket, during your lifetime, is the money paid in taxes. In many countries, taxes can be more than 50% of the income earned. These include the GST, Income Tax, Custom Duties, Excise Duties, Service Tax, Sales Tax, Capital Gains Tax, Stamp Duties and Estate Duties etc.

You may not even be aware of some of the taxes you pay because they are cut at the very source— before you get paid or they get added to the price of goods that you buy on a daily basis. If you add them all up, taxes can take away anything ranging from 40-75% of all that you earn.

Financially intelligent people use investment vehicles and tax saving strategies to save on these taxes. Money saved from taxes through proper planning and invested sensibly can make even a modest earner into a millionaire many times over.

Most financially uneducated people will try and hide their income to save on taxes, and eventually, get in trouble with the law. They will try and save dollars by not consulting an astute accountant and setting up proper structures to save legitimately on taxes.

To grow financially, one has to provide their income details and their turnover: when you do that, you become liable to pay tax. Proper tax planning – not tax avoidance – is the route financially intelligent people take.

Structures for Asset Protection and Tax Planning

This is a very important component of financial intelligence. You should protect your wealth even as you earn. Things, sometimes, can go wrong even with the right knowledge and intentions because no one can have full control over their environment or future events. There is an unknown element in each financial decision we take.

Rich people set up proper structures for asset protection and tax planning before they start. Yes, there is a cost involved in setting up these structures at the beginning, especially at a time when the business or the entity is not generating any income. Normally the cost involved is very small and will pay itself hundred times over if set up correctly. It will also make you sleep better at night.

Risk and Risk Management

Most people refrain from starting a business or investing somewhere because they feel that there is a huge risk involved. What appears like a risk to an untrained mind is like a cake walk for the financially intelligent. This is because they understand those risks and take adequate steps to insure that risk.

I sailed around the world in a 40 ft. yacht. My friends and family thought I had put myself at great risk in such a small boat but I had trained hard and was a knowledgeable sailor. I understood and respected the sea in all its moods.

To me, sailing that boat was safe and an enjoyable experience that enriched me as a person.

Life itself is a risk! The fact that we are born and continue to live is a risky business. We travel by cars and airplanes that can meet with accidents. The human body is fragile. It can give in to cancer, heart failure or a stroke at any stage.

Then there are natural disasters that can strike us at any moment: earthquakes, tsunamis, volcanoes, fires or even a strike from an asteroid can take our lives away in an instance.

Added to this, man has created enough disasters for himself in the form of wars, nuclear power, global warming and terrorism. We cover our risks in daily life by taking prudent decisions and by insuring our health, life and property.

The same can be done in our financial lives. In today's world, every financial risk can be insured. There is a premium involved but this can be an expense that can be taken into account into the cost of running a business or investment. Financially intelligent people not only take out insurances, but also have an exit policy in place for every decision they take. They have business structures in place so that their personal wealth is not touched even if businesses or investments fail.

Robert Kiyosaki rightly put it: "*It is never the business or an investment that is risky. It is always the businessman or the investor who is the risk*." It is our lack of financial knowledge that causes the risk. We get carried away by our emotions of fear and greed, which cause the risk. Risk can be controlled and even eliminated through proper knowledge and insurance.

The biggest risk in life is to remain poor and to have no assets. An even bigger risk in life is to think that someone else will come to our rescue in the hour of need: be it the government, family or friends.

The best thing in life is to rely on our own strength and take steps to become not only financially secure but rich. We have a responsibility towards our family and loved ones to cater for their wellbeing, growth and emergencies in life. The real risk is in not taking timely action to make them financially secure. Avoiding risks to improve one's financial future is just an excuse.

Key Skills of Financially Intelligent People

Financially intelligent people have certain key skills that make them rich. Unfortunately, these key skills are not the focus of what is taught in our schools and colleges.

Creative Thinking

We live in an information age. Most of the times, our minds are overloaded with information; be it the television, the internet, mobile phones or many books and magazines. There is so much information available and very little time to process and digest it. Creative thinking suffers as a result.

A problem solving and creative mind knows where to look for information, and process the data towards a predetermined useful end. An undisciplined mind will waste hundreds of hours in non-productive conversation over the phone or surfing the net lacking focus.

Discipline and focus release the mind from information overload. Only a restive, inward looking and a meditative mind can think creatively and solve problems.

Negotiating

In life, to get what we want, we have to negotiate. We have to get the other party to agree to our terms and conditions. We have to have the skills to change their initial responses: from a "No" to a "Yes." We have to learn the art of compromising for the betterment of both parties.

Communicating

There can be no successful business transaction without proper communication skills. Forget about business development, even marriages and friendships rescind when there is a communication breakdown. You will not achieve your desired results, so long as you are not able to communicate your point of view.

Selling and Marketing

For most people, selling a product or an idea has horrible connotations. It involves rejection, which most people find hard to swallow. The basic truth is that there can be no wealth creation without selling a product or an idea. Profits are generated and encashed once they're sold.

You cannot be successful in any walk of life without being skilled in selling. When you walk into a job interview, you are selling your skills, talents and personality. Even successful dating involves selling your charm, beauty, inner qualities and character.

It is not selling that is difficult: it is the fear of rejection that one has to conquer. Ask any successful entrepreneur and he will tell you that marketing and selling together constitute the oxygen of any business.

Mathematical Mind

Investment and business is about numbers. Basic knowledge of mathematics and accounting is essential to develop a financial mindset. There is no calculus or higher mathematics involved, but basic knowledge is essential.

Emotional Intelligence

We are human beings and emotions play a big part in how we react to the events occurring in our lives. Unfortunately, we cannot control everything that is happening in the world but we can control our reactions to the events that affect us.

Money can be a very emotional thing. If you don't believe me, just visit a stock exchange market and dispassionately observe people and their behavior. How fear and greed take over our rational thinking, how jealous and angry we can get when it comes to money!

Lack of an emotional intelligence causes internal friction in our minds, which saps our energy to do more productive work. There is an internal dialogue which takes place within our minds continuously. There is strife and irritation in our heads if our internal value system is in conflict with our conscious mind. It is only when both are in tune that there is peace within, and our energy levels explode.

What is Emotional Intelligence?

Our emotions emerge from the subconscious. Emotional intelligence accounts for our ability to change unconscious reactions to a conscious response. It means: to perceive and understand emotion, integrate emotion to facilitate thought, and to regulate emotions to promote personal and financial growth.

There is a verse in the Upanishads (sacred Indian text) that states, "If you know a lump of clay then you will know about all the clay in the universe." This means that if you know and understand your own mind, then you will understand all the minds in the universe. All minds function in a similar manner. All our basic human and emotional needs are the same.

To improve our emotional intelligence, we have to bring more and more of our subconscious into conscious examination. Knowledge of the self is the most important step towards improving our emotional intelligence.

Wealth Creation is 90% psychology and only 10% strategy. We have to make internal changes and adjustments to our thinking process that is governed to a very large extent through our emotions, before we can go out and start making money. Changing our psychological foundations is the difficult part, once that is done, creating wealth is a cakewalk.

Spiritual Intelligence

It is essential to understand that we do not live only on one plane of existence. Firstly, there is the material world which we can see, feel and understand. This is the gross or outer cover of life. We aspire for material success and possessions in this world.

Then there is the mind which has two parts: the conscious and the subconscious part. We can't see it, but we know it is there because we can think and dream. The reality of this mind can be entirely different from the real world because it can imagine, dream and be creative.

Finer still is our spirit. Science can't prove it, but we know it is there. It is the unifying force of the universe. It is the underlying principle of life and existence. It unites and not divides. It connects everything in this universe.

At the level of the spirit, we are all one without any differentiation. It is an all-knowledgeable force that permeates into every living or non-living thing. It is also the source of all joy and bliss in this universe. You may call it soul, God or by any other name. It is a reality we cannot deny because at some level we can sense it.

Human spirit is the creative life force of this universe. Most people do not realize that whatever happens in the material world is the printout of the happenings in our spiritual and mental world. Creative people understand this fact and they dip their minds into the cosmos' intelligence to solve their problems and get new ideas.

What is Spiritual Intelligence?

The best definition of spiritual intelligence that I have found is by Frances Vaughan, who states:

"Spiritual intelligence is concerned with the inner life of mind and spirit and its relationship to being in the world. It emerges as consciousness evolves into an ever-deepening awareness of matter, life, body, mind, soul, and spirit. Spiritual intelligence, then, is more than individual mental ability. It appears to connect the personal to the transpersonal and the self to spirit. Spiritual intelligence goes beyond conventional psychological development. In addition to self-awareness, it implies awareness of our relationship to the transcendent, to each other, to the earth and all

beings. Spiritual intelligence opens the heart, illuminates the mind, and inspires the soul, connecting the individual human psyche to the underlying ground of being. Spiritual intelligence can be developed with practice and can help a person distinguish reality from illusion. It may be expressed as love, wisdom, and service."

There are two important things to understand: even the subtlest of movement in the spiritual mind can change things dramatically for the better in the subconscious and the conscious mind, with a resulting effect in the material world.

A thought impulse originating from the spirit can change our whole life. We only have to learn how to trigger that impulse. Secondly, as we gain spiritual intelligence, it harmonizes us with the rest of nature because it a unifying force. This is very important to us in the material world.

It is our sense of conflict in the material world that saps our energy. If we are in harmony then a powerful energy source explodes within us. This has as huge impact on our success in the material world, which is why developing spiritual intelligence is so important to our success.

Abundance of the Universe

Most people feel that to become rich you have to compete for the limited resources that are available in the material world. The act to acquire something in the material world means that you are denying something to the weaker. They abhor the idea that the rich exploit the helpless poor to build their financial empire, which creates a feeling of guilt that holds us back from becoming rich.

Many politicians have won elections exploiting this feeling of guilt and using the theory of social injustice. There is nothing further from the truth because the universe is not limited but abundant. There is no shortage. It is limited only by our restrictive minds.

Our universe is fundamentally abundant. It holds not millions, but billions of undiscovered thoughts, ideas and resources. Each thought, each idea can find resources that are worth billions of dollars.

Just look at the past: there was no television, radio or telecommunications industry before radio waves were discovered. Today, these are huge industries churning out billions of dollars and providing millions of jobs. The person who discovered this one idea – uncovered one secret of the universe – made millions of people wealthy. He did not take anything from the poor but elevated many from the poverty trap.

The same is true of nuclear energy, internet and thousands of new technologies and millions of ideas that are yet to be discovered. Even a very small idea can generate millions for us. We have to open our minds to understand the abundance of the universe.

"Out of abundance he took abundance and still abundance remained."

- Upanishads

The only truth about the universe: it is abundant!

If we embrace such an attitude, blessings and opportunities will follow. It is only limited minds that think that we compete for resources. It is the crab mentality that insinuates pulling others down to succeed.

In fact, truth is just the opposite. We succeed when we help others to succeed. There is abundance in this universe.

Darwin's theory of 'Survival of the fittest' only applies to the animal world. We humans have risen from rest of the animals because of our ability to co-operate and form societies for greater good. It is only fools who think that we are fighting for limited resources in order to survive.

Understanding abundance grows our financial, emotional and spiritual intelligence.

Honesty and Integrity

It is impossible to create long term wealth through dishonest means. The moment you become dishonest you fall out of sync with humanity and the rule of law. You will waste your creative energy fighting with your business partners, competitors, taxmen, customers and employees. Lies breed more lies. Truth and law will eventually catch up with you.

By being honest and leading a life of integrity, you will not only avoid any potential conflicts but generate goodwill that will have a multiplier effect in your wealth creation process. It is difficult to understand why people cheat at times and get violent and get in trouble with the law. In the process, they get entangled in fights, time consuming and expensive law suits, when it takes only miniscule effort to be honest and develop a financial intelligence to create wealth.

How to Get Out of Comfort Zone

To become rich is not easy and convenient. Getting rich can be very hard work. ***If you are willing to do only what is easy, life will be hard. But if you are willing to do what is hard, life will be easy.*** The rich are always willing to take difficult decisions and act on them whereas the poor take the easy and convenient way out.

To become rich is to step out into the unknown and conquer fear. Exploring new thoughts and ideas and incorporating them into our lives means getting out of that comfort zone we are accustomed to.

Each time you step out of your comfort zone, you conquer uncertainty and fear. This expands the size of your comfort zone. The size of your 'comfort zone' equals the size of your 'wealth zone'. By expanding your comfort zone, you will expand the size of your income and wealth.

The more comfortable you are in your little cocoon, fewer risks you will be willing to take and fewer opportunities will come your way. The more contracted you become with fear, fewer people you will meet, and fewer new strategies will you try.

If you are willing to stretch and expand your financial, emotional and spiritual intelligence, the size of your comfort zone will increase and you will attract and hold more income and wealth. The minute you become comfortable, you stop growing.

A moment of fear freezes you for eternity. Being comfortable and fearful has killed more ideas, opportunities, more action and more growth than everything else combined.

The human mind is the greatest soap-opera script writer in history. It plays and replays the greatest dramas—full of tragedies and disasters that never happened and probably never will. Mark Twain said it best: "*I've had thousands of problems in my life, most of which never happened*."

Training and managing our minds out of fear and worries is the most important skill that we will ever develop. We have the power to run our thoughts. We will turn into a failure if we allow our uncontrolled thoughts to dictate our actions.

We have the ability to cancel any thought that does not support our growth process. We have to choose and install self-empowering thoughts. We have the power to control our minds and choose the actions that make us mentally, emotionally, financially and spiritually strong.

Robert Allen said something very profound: "**No thought lives in our head rent- free**." This means if we have fear and negativity in our minds, we will have to pay in terms of money, in energy, in time, in health and in happiness. If we have to move forward then we have to control and expand our mental state. We have to overcome our hesitancy and fears and re-write the script that governs our life.

You can be a millionaire in the next 24 months or sooner, if you can overcome the fear that holds you back.

Can we Eliminate Fear through Knowledge?

The answer is no. The process to perfect our financial, emotional and spiritual intelligence may take years. Our knowledge and training can reduce fear to a very large extent but cannot totally eliminate it.

There will always be grey areas in our knowledge and fear of the unknown will make us hesitant from taking an action.

Act we must, despite our fears, because without action there is no wealth. Every decision in this world is taken with incomplete knowledge. We may try and cover most ground to reduce risk but complete knowledge of the future events and forestalling results is impossible.

We have to make decisions that affect our financial futures in spite of the fear that shackles our minds. This is where the leap of faith comes in: our spiritual intelligence gives us that faith. Courage means to act in spite of fear.

President Franklin D. Roosevelt said it best in his inaugural speech of 1933: *"The only thing we have to fear is fear itself."*

Fear is a natural emotion, and one which we experience with any endeavor we make, as long as we are alive. However, the choice to overcome that fear is ours to make, and will be the determining factor as to whether we fail or we succeed.

I remember seeing a war film wherein a soldier approaches his officer and confesses: "**Sir, I am terribly scared of going into combat.**" The officer gives the soldier a knowing look and says so wisely, "**They must have forgotten to tell you in training school that courage only comes after you face your fears.**"

Where there is success, there will always be the threat of failure. You can't have a victory when there is no threat of defeat—that's just reality. If this was not true, there would be no such thing as competitive sports: there would be no Olympics, there would be no Super Bowl, and there would be no Heavyweight Champion titles. Success is about defeating failure.

Knowledge is a big help in eliminating fear. But no one acts out of perfect knowledge. There is an element of uncertainty in every decision we make. It is not necessary to try and get rid of fear; success is about acting in spite of our fear.

Fears, when examined in the light of knowledge, are no longer fears. The impressions of financial fear and loss that are so deeply embedded in our hearts and mind begin to reduce with an increase in our financial, emotional and spiritual intelligence. Once this irrational fear is removed from the heart and the mind, the path for gaining riches is cleared.

It can take years to first erase and then rewrite the script in our subconscious that will set us onto path of wealth creation. Our fears and attitudes come in the way of our knowledge progression because they contaminate our processors.

If we had better attitudes and fewer fears, then our mind's processor will not be tainted; acquisition of new thoughts and ideas will be that much better. Once we have more knowledge, then we can better understand our attitudes and fears that cause hindrance in our journey of becoming rich.

The endless cycle of filtration and purifying of knowledge continues: we move from less knowledge to more knowledge and break one chain at a time that ties us to poverty. This can take an awfully long time. Fortunately, there are ways and means to short cut the process if we make a conscious effort to hasten the process.

How to Re-wire to Become an Enlightened Millionaire

The first step to becoming an enlightened millionaire is to get the mindset of a millionaire. **Process of wealth creation is 90% psychology and only 10% strategy**. Most people fail to become rich because they want to learn the strategy and not focus on changing their psychology.

To be a winner, you have to have the mindset of a winner. The inner change has to precede the external outcome. We have known this since the time we were kids: a certain set of rules enlisted by our parents, teachers and peers need to be followed. We believed in them because they were given to us in love and in good faith. Some of the rules that were ingrained in us were from people whose mindsets were steeped in poverty. We can't blame them because one or two generations back, most of our families were poor and struggling to survive.

As the world moves towards greater prosperity, we have to learn the new set of rules that govern the rich. The new rules are easy to learn only if you have an open mind to learn and succeed. We have to rewrite the script, or order a new set of rules that govern our lives.

It is not sufficient to get rid of the old impressions from our minds – it is only the first step. The old script was a baggage that held us back from becoming rich and forbade us from living life to its full potential.

To succeed, we have to re-write the old script to that of the 'Enlightened Millionaire' in our minds. This is the inner principle of wealth creation. Once the new script is written, it is a point of no return. You can never be middle-class or poor again even if you lose your entire wealth and have to restart from a scratch.

The millionaire mindset once achieved, is a non-destructive commodity. It stays with you for life. You can lose your millions but you will always bounce back. You are a millionaire because of your mindset.

Re-write the Script from Your Heart

The motivation to re-write the script has to originate from the heart because the mind has its own set of limitations— it is always the heart that rules. Whenever there is a conflict between the heart and the mind, it is always the heart that wins. A transformational change can occur only if it comes from the heart. Incremental increase of knowledge can take place in the mind but transformation of the mind can take place only if the heart is involved.

The heart, as we know it, is our subconscious. How can we involve our subconscious into the wealth creation process? To do that, we have to understand what triggers our heart and soul. We have so many desires buried within our subconscious. We have to simply uncover and trigger one or more of these desires into the wealth creation process.

To involve the heart means to find the predominant motivating triggers and activating them. You cannot live someone else's dream— you have to find your own.

The secret of wealth creation lies in finding your own triggers that drive your heart and soul. The nobler your trigger, the greater are your chances of success. A higher and better cause gets more people involved and your chances towards success increases exponentially.

A callous desire normally results in conflicting situations with a lesser chance of success. However, there is nothing wrong in following any of your dreams because once a dream is satisfied; there is always a next dream that will trigger you towards greater cause and effect. It is an evolutionary process. It is however, prudent on what you set your heart on and as Emerson rightly pointed out, "*it surely will be yours.*"

To understand our triggers, we have to apply the *S.S.S* formula explained by Ron Holland in his book Talk and Grow Rich. According to him, to understand our subconscious we have to follow **SILENCE, STILLNESS AND SOLITUDE**. The secret to understanding these triggers of our mind lies in meditation – in silence, stillness and solitude or the S.S.S. When you become quiet, it just dawns on you.

Sometimes, an external stimulus is needed to activate the internal process... much like the process of falling in love. It is the beauty of an external person that activates love and desire in our hearts.

Similarly, experience of suffering can ignite compassion in our hearts. At times by putting ourselves in situations and gaining the right stimuli, we can understand the triggers that operate within our subconscious.

You will be able to re-write the '**enlightened millionaire**' script much faster if you understand your dreams and inner motivation. So take time out to understand these dreams and write them on a piece of paper—it will hasten the process. If you know your objective, then the path to success becomes easier to tread on.

The Butterfly Effect

To bring about internal change in our attitude, we have to understand the butterfly effect. The phrase refers to the idea that the flapping of a butterfly's wings might create tiny changes in the atmosphere that ultimately cause a tornado to appear (or prevent a tornado from appearing.)

The flapping wing represents a small change in the initial condition of the system, which causes a chain of events leading to large-scale phenomena. This implies that a small change in the initial condition may produce large variations in the long-term behavior of the system.

We do not have to do anything spectacular to help change our script to an 'enlightened millionaire's mindset,' but we can make small changes to alter the initial condition that can change the long term trajectory of our lives. In the succeeding paragraphs we will discuss some suggestions that can trigger a butterfly effect. You may apply some or all of them to change the outcome of your life.

Control the Inputs to Your Mind

To change the script of our life, we have to understand how the script is written in the mind. The script in the mind is written through thoughts, words, feelings and actions. Each one of them is very important as they leave indelible impressions on the mind. If we can learn to control our thoughts, words, feelings and actions in the present, then we have the power to change our future.

Power of Thoughts and Words

Thoughts are subtle but important because they are the starting point of the process. But once they become words, they have tremendous impact on both our internal and external reality. If you don't believe me, just call someone a bastard and your teeth will come out. Similarly, words of love and kindness will evoke a totally different – but positive – response.

Words, both written and oral, have tremendous power. They leave a deep impression on the mind. We are responsible for our thoughts and words and have to learn to control them. To have the millionaire's mindset, we have to snap out of any negative thought or action.

We have to read or listen to the words of successful and enlightened wealth creators. We have to place ourselves in their company and associate with them so that their words may influence us and change our script.

To illustrate this point: write down the names of five people with whom you spend your maximum time. Now, study their profile. Are they rich… entrepreneurs? Are they wealth creators? Or are they limited in their vision of job security? If you hang around with poor, negative and unsuccessful people then that is what the future beholds for you. You are writing the script of poverty.

To write the script of an enlightened wealth creator, you have to seek the right company to influence your mind. You have to change your reading habits and listen to lectures and tapes of highly successful people. You have to learn to speak the language of the rich.

Your script change will gain added momentum when words of success and positivity start flowing from your pen and mouth. The words you think, write and speak have greater impact on your mind than the words you receive from others.

Initially, the control of thoughts and words will look artificial and irksome. It may not come naturally but it can be done. It has to be a conscious effort. You have to start by watching our thoughts and words, and speak with good purpose only.

Through a change in your reading habits and allowing your mind to be influenced by the right associations, you can accelerate the process and completely change your script to that of an enlightened millionaire. It is a small change in the initial condition that is required to create the 'Butterfly Effect'. And once the effect takes place, it becomes a part of your inner nature.

There can be no Change without Action

Thoughts and words have to manifest into action lest there will be no change. Moreover, action and events in the external world leave a far greater impact on your mind than thoughts and words.

Thoughts are the starting point. They are subtle but create the least impact. Once they manifest into words, they create a much greater impact on the mind. And once words manifest into action, they have the most powerful impact on our minds and the outer world.

To understand this point, let us take the example of an inventor; he thinks of a new invention or product. It is just a concept in his mind. He does not wish to pursue the idea further. It dies a natural death. If he decides to writes a paper on the subject and speak at a few seminars, it not only clarifies his thought process but also starts influencing the minds of others. Now if he takes action to create the new product, then it will impact his future in financial terms but will also leave an impact on those who use or associate with the product.

Actions, though a result of thoughts and words, can prove to be a more powerful instrument of change, as they have a greater impact on the script.

A huge number of people, who read the right kind of books, listen to tapes and attend seminars but take no action. They wish to acquire complete knowledge and eliminate risk before embarking on the process of wealth creation. That perfect situation never comes because what future beholds, no one knows—it is always full of uncertainties.

An educated mind can eliminate some eventualities but, "the fog of war will always remain." All successful commanders know when to act despite being provided with limited information on the enemy. Inaction certainly leads to defeat. The same is true in the world of finance.

If you do not act then you cannot make any money. There is saying: "***once you put your money in line, knowledge will come that much faster.***" There is no faster way to rewrite the enlightened millionaire's script than to take action. There is no teacher like experience. Think big but start small. Learn to take a few successful steps before you can start to run.

Knowledge + Action = Wealth

Action is the key. Without action, all your knowledge turns to waste. Be bold and take action. Boldness has genius, power and magic.

Whatever your inspiration or dream—act on it. The most fundamental principle of wealth creation is to take action. No one can ever reach the stage of complete knowledge to overcome fear.

All wealth creators have to learn to manage fear. In every decision you take, there will be an element of uncertainty. There has to be a leap of faith as the information required for decision making is never adequate. Act, you must, in good faith and intelligence! Inaction will keep you tied to poverty.

Once you start taking action, your experience and confidence will increase. There is no better teacher than experience. A few successful steps will change your future. You will rewrite wealth script ten times faster with action.

Feelings make your Words and Actions Stronger

Words when spoken with feelings are a hundred times stronger than those spoken with no heart in them. Have you enjoyed a song that has been sung with passion? It takes a totally new dimension. The same is true for action when it is backed by positive emotion.

When there is joy in action, there is no burden on the task at hand. If the heart is not there, it becomes a tedious job. To rewrite your script your heart has to be in it. Without feelings, there will be no joy or beauty in your script. It will be very difficult to rewire.

Uncovering the power of your emotions will release a tidal wave of change in your life. When there is feeling of love in your words and actions, you will be transformed.

To understand your genius and passion, you have to be still. Through silent introspection, self-reflection and meditation you increase your self-awareness. As your self-awareness increases, you will understand what your heart really wants. Don't chase the artificial or what the world wants you to be. Be true to yourself and your inner beliefs and success will follow you.

Clarity of Purpose

There has to be clarity of purpose when rewriting your script or it will be unintelligible. If there is no clarity then you yourself will not be able to read your script, let alone understand it.

Firstly, there has to be a decision that resonates with: "*I will be an enlightened millionaire.*"

Then, you have to state your intention and commit it in writing. Writing your statement brings more clarity to your thought process.

Lastly, you have to announce it to the whole world that you are going to be an enlightened millionaire by a particular date—tell your friends, family and the whole world about your intentions. It will put pressure on you; instead it will keep you focused. You have to burn your bridges behind you to succeed. Without commitment, there is no clarity.

Goals are very critical to your success. They have to be clearly defined and practically achievable. To keep yourself balanced, you can record different goals in major areas of your life like health, relationships, intellectual, spiritual and financial goals. You have to write them, read them, see them and talk about them in every waking or dreaming moment of your life. You will then see your goals magically materialize into your life.

To become an enlightened millionaire you have to make a decision, state your intention and set goals. You have to live from your goals and think about them day and night.

Clarity and focus in your script will accelerate your pace of growth like nothing else. Can you imagine writing an article without a topic or a heading? The article will be confusing to the readers – it will be unintelligible. Similarly, without stating your goal and intention, your life script will be full of confusion.

To gain clarity you have to state your goals and put them in writing. You have to view and repeat these goals on a daily basis to stay on track and in focus. It looks simply but you will be surprised to learn that over 99% of the population has no stated goals and as a result, drift along in life. To be successful, you have to state your goals clearly and stay focused.

Be Congruent

There is a difference between a goal and an agenda: you can have a clearly stated goal but your hidden agenda can often sabotage that goal.

Our hidden agenda is normally driven by our ego, deep seated prejudices and value systems. Our hidden agendas are like saboteurs who are out to destroy our most well laid plans. We have to find these little saboteurs and convert them to our side.

To succeed you have to be congruent. You have to align your mind, body and spirit to a single purpose. Ask any top athlete. At the crucial point of winning-losing, they have their mind and body dissolves into one. There is no thought but only singularity of purpose. This singularity of purpose makes them champions.

The greatest loss of energy takes place because of attrition in the mind. When there is conflict of goals with our value system the script gets corrupted. We have to turn deep within ourselves to understand our hidden prejudices and value systems. We have to either bring in change to our inner attitudes or modify our goals to bring them into alignment with our core values. Without this, we will be working at cross purposes that will be deterrent to our success.

By little observation you can find out if there is a conflict within your mind and belief system.

People who complain of lethargy usually suffer from some kind of an inner conflict. One way to resolve such a conflict is through understanding the flow of energy. When everything is in alignment, there will be no noise and friction in the mind. If you are congruent, there will be explosion of energy within your system. Your script will then have clarity and sense of its purpose.

Transformational Change

Here we are not talking about increments in your script – we are talking of how you can achieve a quantum jump that can transform you instantly. It is transformational learning as against informational learning that is predominant in our educational system that defines our script.

Informational learning is passive; teachers talk and students listen. It is about memorization, examinations and grades. Teachers talk about subjects on which they have theoretical knowledge, but lack practical experience—such an education can never be inspirational.

Transformational learning is about self-discovery. The student is given an inspirational stimulus by a mentor who has traveled the path and has discovered the answers to the problems through his experience.

All the knowledge to become a millionaire is already within you. No one can teach you how to become rich. Someone can only inspire you to awaken every cell in your body that will cry out that you were born to be rich and free, and to live a life of abundance. It is your natural state.

Transformation occurs when the right stimulus is given to awaken what is inside us and our script changes instantaneously.

Mentors

The shortcut to transformational knowledge is to find a mentor; they are invaluable! They have travelled the path and they have the knowledge. They will stir you in their presence. A word of advice from them will transform you. It will be a life changing experience that no book, DVD or tape can provide.

Where can you find Mentors?

The truth is you cannot find a mentor until you are ready. The day you are ready a mentor will appear. A little preparation is required at your end to receive a mentor.

No one can inspire you until you are ready to be inspired. No one can change you until you desire the change. No one can make you rich until you want to be rich. When this happens, a mentor will appear in your life and take you forward in leaps.

There are mentors all around us but we don't see them because we are not mentally prepared for them. We associate ourselves with losers, time wasters, frivolous and non-productive people. How can we eject magnetic waves to attract successful people?

To gain some magnetic power, we have to initially force ourselves to the presence of people who emanate powerful doses of the magnetic energy we want. Association is a very powerful thing. If you associate with the right kind of people, you will be subjected to the right kind of energy fields. This will transform you. You will also become a magnet attracting the right kind of people. There is nothing new in it – it is the basic law of attraction.

"The soul attracts that which it secretly harbors, that which it loves, and also that which it fears. It reaches the height of its cherished aspirations. It falls to the level of its chastened desires – and circumstances are the means by which the soul receives its own." As a Man Thinketh by James Allen (1864 - 1912)

A mentor carries a hundred times stronger energy field. He can transform us to a different level instantly. However, we will receive the energy only once we are mentally prepared to accept the energy.

Thoughts have an energy that attracts like energy. A mentor will come to us when we are ready and not a day before that. We have to develop our thoughts (conscious and unconscious,) emotions, beliefs and actions to a certain level in order to attract the positive energy from a mentor.

If you study the lives of wealth creators, you will find they have been mentored not by one but several mentors at different periods of their lives. A mentor will not only fill the gaps in your knowledge but will inspire you to new levels of achievement, which you think is not possible. They will change your thought process and internal script.

Is it expensive to get mentors? Not necessarily. If you are serious and dedicated, you can get mentored for free. All masters take on assistants to do their 'grunt work,' so that they can leverage their time. You can volunteer to become their apprentice.

There is a Chinese proverb that goes like: "*A single conversation across the table with a wise man is worth a month's study of books.*" You can invite a mentor to a meal—it works like a charm.

Final Thoughts

Fears, when examined in the light of knowledge, are no longer fears. The impressions of financial fear and loss that are so deeply embedded in our hearts and mind begin to reduce with an increase in our financial, emotional and spiritual intelligence. Once this irrational fear is removed from the heart and the mind, the path for gaining riches is cleared.

The purpose of this book will be served if it helps in educating and help morph enlightened people who create wealth the right way, preserve wealth the right way and ultimately, use their wealth for the greater good of humanity. This process leads to seeking a higher purpose in life and its fulfillment. I hope and pray that to some extent, that purpose is served. If you have read to this point, I thank you with gratitude in my heart and hope you succeed in creating true wealth that helps not only you and your family but entire humanity.

If you liked the book and gained some knowledge that will be useful to you in life, then please leave an honest review to help others find this book. It will be a small effort on your part, but an act of charity that may help in changing few lives for the better. We thank you in advance for your help.

This book is about fundamental principles of wealth creation that can be applied to any business or investing strategy. At <u>Wealth Creation Academy</u>, we teach multitude ways to generate passive income, which includes: real estate investing, digital publishing, affiliate marketing, multi-level marketing and investing in forex, commodities, and shares by copying experienced traders that need very little of time. You may like to get started with some of the strategies depending on your budget and time.

Other Books by the Authors

Praveen Kumar has authored several bestselling books. Please visit his website **http://praveenkumarauthor.com/** for more information

About the Authors

Praveen Kumar was abandoned by his father at the age of fourteen and joined the Navy at tender age of fifteen where education, roof and free food were guaranteed.

In order to understand the root cause of suffering he turned towards philosophy and religion. After 10 years of soul searching and meditation he understood that 'life is 'and material and spiritual world are closely interwoven. You cannot live in one without the other.

Praveen was highly successful in the Navy, where he successfully commanded submarines, sailed around the world in a yacht and received gallantry award for his contribution to the Navy.

Despite his success in the Navy, Praveen realized that lack of financial security for his family was one of key root causes of his suffering, resulting from his childhood deprivation. To improve his financial standing, Praveen took pre-mature retirement from the Navy to build his financial future through investing in Real Estate. The decision to educate on financial matters paid off, and today he and his wife are comfortably retired on six-figure passive income.

His aim is to help others create wealth in an enlightened way and empower them to live a healthy and happy life. He dedicates his time to write books and articles on financial and spiritual matters.

Prashant graduated with distinction from Auckland University as a computer engineer and later completed his MBA from the world's leading institution - INSEAD. During his successful corporate career, he worked for the most reputable consulting firms in the world - BCG &

Deloitte - and represented New Zealand on Prime Minister-led trade missions to South East Asian countries.

After successfully generating income through his passive investments in property and stocks, Prashant decided to team up with his father to help people transform their lives through the leverage of financial education.

Their website http://wealth-creation-academy.com/ is devoted to teaching people how to create Multiple Streams of Passive Income through investing in real estate, online marketing and creating digital products

Made in United States
Orlando, FL
27 August 2022

21611688R00048